Where It Hurts

Where It Hurts

Poems by

Jon Ballard

© 2025 Jon Ballard. All rights reserved.
This material may not be reproduced in any form, published,
reprinted, recorded, performed, broadcast,
rewritten, or redistributed without
the explicit permission of Jon Ballard.
All such actions are strictly prohibited by law.

Cover design by Shay Culligan
Cover image by Jan Canty
Author photo by Natalie Ballard

ISBN: 978-1-63980-714-7

Kelsay Books
502 South 1040 East, A-119
American Fork, Utah 84003
Kelsaybooks.com

for Betsy

And here—
where I twisted the heart when I thought
I could burn the pain away,
when I thought it wasn't mine.

—Lawrence Raab
from "The Island of Lost Souls"

Acknowledgments

Grateful acknowledgment is made to the publications in which the following poems first appeared, sometimes in different forms:

Autumn Sky Poetry: "Late November Dusk"
Barnwood Magazine: "Readying the Rag"
BlazeVOX: "End of the World," "Root Canal," "Time Capsule"
Boxcar Poetry Review: "Trees Make You Think of Other Things"
DMQ Review: "Old Grove," "Book People," "Two Player Games"
Fifth Wednesday Journal: "Neighbors," "The Shadow Throwers"
Finishing Line Press (Chapbook): "Somewhere Between"
Great Lakes Review: "Stalled Trains at Paddock Street," "Reaching Shore," "Last Day Together," "These Unaccountable Moods"
Grey Sparrow Journal: "Always a Musical," "After the Storm"
Halfway Down the Stairs: "Note to Self"
La Fenetre: "The Cliff Divers of La Quebrada"
Melee: "The Hired Man"
New Mexico Poetry Review: "Provincial Cemetery with Figures"
Northwest Indiana Literary Journal: "Lucky Bastard"
San Pedro River Review: "Where It Hurts," "Playing Your Part, 1964"

Contents

I—It Starts as a Joke

Letter of Appreciation	17
Root Canal	18
Readying the Rag	19
Yes, No, Maybe	20
After Dinner, We Advance	21
Time Capsule	22
Playing Your Part, 1964	23
Note to Self	25
The Hired Man	26
Last Day Together	27
Always a Musical	29
Assassin	30
End of the World	31
Late November Dusk	32
It Starts as a Joke	33
Left to Wonder	34
Book People	36
Visitation	37
Mid-Year Reset	39

II—No Rest for the Weary

Neighbors	43
Old Grove	44
These Unaccountable Moods	45
Trees Make You Think of Other Things	46
The Shadow Throwers	47
Provincial Cemetery with Figures	48
Stalled Trains at Paddock Street	49

The Cliff Divers of La Quebrada	50
Looking Down on Tepoztlán	51
Two-Player Games	52
After the Storm	53
Somewhere Between	54
No Rest for the Weary	56
Testimony	57
Where It Hurts	58
The Fall	59
Having Learned Nothing	61
Doing Damage	64
Lucky Bastard	65
Busted Compass	67
Shaping the Scene	69
The Wars of Repetition	72
Reaching Shore	73

I—It Starts as a Joke

Letter of Appreciation

I won't bother citing the usual suspects,
those gray gods or earth spirits, or the kinder
friends and family who do their boulder-breaking
on my behalf behind the scenes, often
in unstinting silence. Though let's be fair
and perhaps ever-so-cynical: their silence
can sometimes seem little better than
the pat-themselves-on-the-back stomaching
of my ceaseless woes. Nor would I bother
to give the rockstar philosophers
and scientists of the day any due,
the way their keen but ever-doomier
decrees whip up my already howling
inner weather. And you can just forget
about me lauding my old foxhound, who
truth be told does his one job loving me
with great aplomb—maestro of unreserved
nuzzling that he's become—but doesn't
know or seem to appreciate that it's
only my fickle human regard that gives
his beast-life meaning. Or whose naughty
habit of sporadic escape I often excuse,
running off after one scent or another,
then hours later, dog-tired by the side
of the road, picked up by the police
like a common criminal. Returned to me
oblivious and unrepentant, yet galling
in his readiness to nuzzle, not out of
some furry sense of duty, but because.

Root Canal

The pictures of cheetahs
on the office walls are
strangely comforting, as
if nothing so lithe or beautiful
would stay here unwillingly.
Your dentist sees you staring.
"Family," he says, without irony.
Your spittle jets forth, gurgles
like an antelope's with
a cheetah's jaws on its neck.
Through the window, tips
of bare trees prick gray sky—
distal clouds, like your mouth
(you imagine) locally anesthetized,
suffering the instruments
of intrusion but none of the pain.
The masked dental assistant
calls you a real trooper, tugs
your dulled lip like flaccid sex.
Her eyes monastic, cat-blue.

Readying the Rag

Come to think of it, we're not
lost, says the dust, having returned
home to the coffee table, cresting

now on that morning's water rings,
squatting on the broad banks
of the *Big Book of Rivers & Streams*

and in the (dust)bowl of hand-
painted apples and pears. Tribes
of other grime loiter in the air,

unsure of where to come to rest,
noticing the woman of the house
with her cleaning rag and spray can

of Pledge—O vision of apocalypse!
Then the phone rings, and she begins
to laugh in her mad, hysterical

way, pure henchwoman, laughing
and listening, readying the rag,
waiting for all the dust to settle.

Yes, No, Maybe

I should never revisit certain errors of the heart. Loitering yet again under the transom of desire. At the blast door of wanting. Then no matter how hard I shoulder it, never crashing in. Noting how bloodied my ceaselessly rapping knuckles get. How many hours I can stand there fancying what is hidden inside, just beyond knowing. All that I've already missed and all that I haven't yet missed but will. Whole years like mortal wounds bleeding out this way. Recalling how I once took *maybe* for an answer because it offered hope, however (obviously) false. Better that middling poison than *no's* snake venom—oh I was too young then to die such a death. And what about *yes*, that most terrifying of gifts, the one I could never let myself accept? Convinced nothing that good or true should be so easy to earn. Still in thrall to love's playing-hard-to-get grandeur. Still believing I of all people could never possibly deserve it.

After Dinner, We Advance

to the sofa, electing opposite
ends, but ogling like two people
who know better than to kid
themselves. Though admiring
the ruddy throughline of your
bony parts—knees, elbows, cheeks—
I avert my eyes and gape
instead at the blanched water
ringlets on my coffee table,
the lone white beagle hair on my
black sweater vest, all too aware
the petty god of chagrin is
making yet another house call.
For a while we run the gauntlet
of our nerves, marvel at all
the ways in which the world
has changed since the last time
we did this. We cop to being out
of sorts—alone with each other
on a sofa this way—though both
of us have been here before
in previous lives with wrong
people. I warn you then I'm out
of practice in the art of seduction,
which luckily you hear not as
middle-aged humblebrag, but
as the light comedy of surrender.

Time Capsule

In the rummaging way
of dreams your letter
found me. A twenty-two
cent stamp told how
many years were gone,
though your worn words
scribbled easy toward
a measure of now.

So like you, pilgrim
from my past, to come
again singing such casual
certainty—"I see a beach
party in our future!"—
your silly vision made
faint by heavy years,
arched there on the page

forever where your small
hands decided one
of two folds should be.

Playing Your Part, 1964

I'm straddling your aproned hip—
child-as-clichéd-maternal-prop—
while behind me your hidden arm
surely forms a brace against my
writhing to escape the frame.
Your free hand is caught mid-swipe
tidying claret locks from your brow,
a last-ditch primp for the camera.
And behind us, the backyard midsummer
lush, the lawn overgrown, though
that posed smile of yours flashes wry
no doubt because you've managed
to hide your two big feet in
the ankle-high fescue. One more
part of your body you didn't love.
A body, after two children, your
husband shared in scorning, swindled
he must have reasoned by the false
sureties of virginal splendor.
And your red hair, pale fire against
the picture's ancient shaft of blue
sky, dyed to suit him who had
long ago tired of dishwater blonde.
Think of all such early alterations
of the self. Of all the suspect choices
made by the ever-credulous heart,
and always in the name of love or
some better-than-nothing facsimile.
Think of photographs like this one—
mother holding child—as evidence
of what it was like in those moments
when you still warranted his gaze,

when you were willing to hold any
pose he captured, playing your part
in whatever flimsy story you both
needed that day to tell yourselves.

Note to Self

All your soul talk has tormented
the skin, this sun-shambled wrap.
The frame within creaks at bending

points, nothing the rest of you
can do but grin and bear out
this anguish of bones. Sticky-

note to self: forget the eternal,
focus instead on the steps at your
feet, the door before you, turn

the brass knob, enter the dark shell
of the sky, tumble of stars, smell
of rain far off, moist thread of memory

as if you had lived a thousand
years in many places, though now here
as flesh and bone again, comparing

raindrops of Persia and pacific atoll
and small-town Michigan, sweet haunts
body knows by step, soul by rights.

The Hired Man

I offer him my last bottle
of root beer, exchange
perfunctory words about
the heat-dulled morning,
the pros and cons of gutter-
guards, appraise his gray-tipped
whiskers, his whiskey/root
beer breath, his sweat-soaked
tee-shirt that reads like a droll
epitaph or as simple self-odium
—*Return to sender*—
all the while disguising my pity
as mild interest in his plight.
He's a man happy to be needed,
but not needed too much.
Glad for idle time between jobs:
trout fishing up north, ball-
games, loving two or three
women all at once (whiskered
grin), not getting caught.

Last Day Together

1.

All day hums
of out-of-tune
passersby.
They mean well
enough, and make
the sky
up where
muted clouds are
a refuge.
No rain. Or
rain, but
lucky: only after
errands
which include
stuffing our faces.
Dear bistro.

2.

Love is
only love
if you can't keep it
down. So you say
you'll get
the check if
I'll take
the umbrella.
On the way home
you explain—
if I understand
correctly.

3.

Such strange
obsidian
weather, or
murder of crows.
Clouds
made of sea,
islands of cloud,
my hand
made of small bones
digging
around your
heart ablaze.
This one last
firebreak.

Always a Musical

Doe-eyed girls singing country songs
for us, uneasy yet rapt auditioners
for the coveted role of Most Adorable Child.
We parents, creators of this now decade-long
production of The Happy Family, half-wincing
at the broken harmonies and under-rehearsed
dance routines. Their bedtime-hour long past,
the summer darkness descends like a final
curtain while the girls and now their
mother giggle, amused beyond easy repair.
Happy in the presence of this troika
of pale-skinned beauties, but sullen always
in the pit of my own muddled gut, I can't
help but observe them like a climber
at the summit, keen to get on with the tricky
work of descent. Anxious suddenly, picturing
a future show of their childish grandeur,
but this time a darker bit with faux tears
and fake melodrama. Something, let's
say, where they play sisters who don't
wholly love each other, and where
the parents—aloof and grim as caretakers
of unfixable errors—don't allow bedtimes
to pass unnoticed, let alone such music
in the house, all the silly song-and-dance.

Assassin

There always comes a point at these things when silence intrudes, that ham-fisted chaperone parting you from your darling words, and all that's left to do is abscond to the cash bar: another whisky, cold comfort all the way down, but a definite task by which to busy yourself until the next surly remark can be mustered—impugning, say, the deejay's Motown fixation—before diving into ad hoc sermons on the grim politics of the day, God's gray light eddying over the hall's casement windows like dishwater circling a drain, the burlesque of all these dancing fools with Marvin Gaye in their mouths, belting out *Ain't No Mountain High Enough,* dupes for stirring sentiment, for the easy schmaltz of songs. And now look: bride and groom leading the offkey chorus—he, ardent in his monkey suit, she, lithe in her lacy boho number, as if doyens suddenly in the high art of amorous vows. Unlike you (long-time assassin of the heart, always on the clock), slouched now to better convey ironic distance, half-searching the scrum for your date to tell her you're fed up, you're leaving any minute. To say she can stay all night if she wants, she can sing and dance her bloody heart out.

End of the World

Storefronts refusing the stray
customer: not a single sale
banner or *Yes, we're open* sign.
Glass display cases bare
but for yellowed newspapers
and last season's unsold wares.
All along Main Street the hard
lean of dwarf trees, reluctant
as children tugged in a certain,
undesirable direction. A spilled
applecart of antiques: Bascombe's
Mystery, Stump of the World—
no Red Delicious for miles and miles.
Lovers in the square who haven't
kissed for hours, almost buried now
in gold and crimson maple leaves.
The local mortician pulling up
the dusty miller, hands and knees
in the black beds, getting dirty,
getting good and dirty.

Late November Dusk

Your day whittled down
to nothing, evening puts away
its pocketknife. Last leaves
everywhere jump from their
timber ledges (so near
is the season of resolutions.)
Close by, burning foliage wafts
its brazen signal into the darkness:
city ordinances be damned.
Enjoying that pungency means
conspiring with those felonious
souls three streets due west,
the ones who over-decorate
every Halloween, whose ill-
mannered boys—the gossips
next door assure—will amount
to nothing. You're not a gossip,
but you prefer eavesdropping
to raking this plague of color.
Truth be told, you relish
those indiscreet voices
judging, foretelling, conjuring
like a cauldron of witches,
though decorous in their
enmity, tender even.

It Starts as a Joke

Idle, yes, but stinging: how in our next life we should plan for trouble right from jump street, since trouble follows us wherever we go. But what if your little joke isn't the surefire truth you make it out to be? What if this ballsed-up life of ours begets better sense for the next go-round? Say a Karmic draught carries in some exotic, potent caution, and we *don't* say hello to each other at the party, instead leaving earlier with different, less trouble-adjacent people. Or better still: maybe we both go home solo, for once not fearing the breakage of solitude's minor aftershocks. We become two people leading separate lives, alone in different rooms where we try to ignore the same dogged ache, a pulse at the dim boundaries of our sensory range, like a lost limb's phantom throb. Some vital part of us sacrificed years before in service to an inexplicable, greater good. Even though no one else we meet can ever help us fathom what it was we were trying to accomplish, or what we possibly stood to gain.

Left to Wonder

The way years ago
the bully went soft,
identified with your
victimhood. Or—let's
not be sentimental—
more likely wearied
of your stale panic
in favor of the four-eyed
transfer from Our Lady
of Sissies. Or how
hard dreams quit piercing
you with dread for
the new day's cosmic
wedgie: possible it was
cutting out carbs
and caffeine after eight,
just as the grocery rags
claimed . . . and what about
that brute's surprise
eviction from the flat
above? Carnival dreck
you swore stilt-walked
up there, catapulted, lion-
tamed, deep-fried elephant
ears at all hours—maybe
it *was* your thousand
honeyed prayers before
bedtime that got the job
done, and not all those
unsigned notes slipped

under the super's door
after midnight. Screeds
ominous enough to crook
a ramrod spine, to make
an old bully proud.

Book People

Let's be clear: not any cleverer than the rest. And they can be so bound up in a story's elaborate love knots that little by little they misremember how desire in the real world, lacking a Florentine backdrop, say, might easily prosper—how a *piazza* factors less in amorous schemes than *pizza* ever did. Kinked necks, hands steeped in the fusty-paged tang of shelf-years, eyes trimmed in dollar-store cheaters. Good-for-nothing sorts when the rain is steady and the lamplight near. The rest of us moseyed off, taking our beautiful inside noises to other rooms, keeping a distance that loving them entails.

Visitation

Coming from a direction
that set our compasses reeling,
though a few naysayers
under their breath convinced
he'd started out from a place
no more exotic than the far
end of the block. Others
like me with a dourer bent
quick to claim his was the leaden
gaze of one of those hooked souls
encamped under the viaduct.
Then a charitable couple
among the throng reasoning
he might be the hermit they'd
spied slinking through the back
alleyway on rainy afternoons,
even as their young son
was tugging at the visitor's
shapeless trousers, babbling on
about how he'd seen him change
into a red box kite stuck way up
in the park's biggest tree,
whereupon the boy's hoary
hound began baying, sniffing
(many suspected) the scent
of far off places, of someone
who has gone away and returned
somehow changed. The crowd
astounded by the oracular yowl
of an otherwise daft animal,
even as a fearful consensus
began to build that with a few

dark embellishments the story
of this cryptic arrival in our midst
had all the proper makings
of a blockbuster viral moment—
say the latest bloody installment
from the ongoing solitary-man-
goes-ballistic genre. All assembled
in further agreement that his next
capricious act could be the one
upon which the whole world
gets its first orgasmic chance
to rant or rave, an act possibly
so cracked we might begin to see
his natural affinity for every
human circus to come. The few
optimists among us holding out
instead for a homily on
the central credo of his kind,
which like any clever Venusian
or messiah or even the least
serviceable of gods, should be
to leave us slack-jawed but happy
to be fooled, always wanting more.
To confer upon us the buoyant
feeling that what can't be
understood is nothing at all to fear,
but something soul-stirring
and wondrous indeed.

Mid-Year Reset

Start learning to wear guilt so well
people badger you for the name
of your tailor. One day soon wake
up from a dream that felt real
not because in it you lacked
heroic bravery, but because
you kept your weakest nerve.
On that stellar morning climb out
of the tangled sheets, and instead
of already bearing the weight
of the world's suspicions—as if
the grim night boss came up short
counting the money drawers
and you-know-who was the lone
cashier on shift—let your step be
light as a child's, if not quite that
of the wholly innocent man.
Or, let's say, while staring at him
in the glass who always stares
back, forgo your mulish disdain
for the familiar, ignore the pitched
brow and gaping mouth that
often make a gargoyle out
of him, don't ask under your breath
what he's gone and done with
your happiness. Admit at last
there are no satisfactory answers,
and trust this time that the man
in the mirror, though he could
make up anything to fool you,
loves you too much to even try.

II—No Rest for the Weary

Neighbors

As to taverns of song and joy
morning birds flock to lush,

indulgent maples.
Rain of darker hours

whispers down into
the pores of the earth.

I don't love my neighbors
this dawn after storms.

They are all asleep, still
apostles in their own dreams

of glorious movements.
On waking, they will

forgive themselves fully
their reverie's hubris,

though in the birdsong
they will hear enchantments—

faint, maybe—yet like Odysseus
tied to his mast, they'll listen.

Old Grove

My dream a tree-line, dark
with undue calculations.
The gist: something like my
best age—ten or eleven—
yet stranded and solitary

as a wing-plucked wasp.
Undergrowth like arbutus
but scentless, withering.
The voice I hear is deep
within this gloaming—

a land meant to loathe,
a voice meant to heed.
This old grove tolerates me:
my indolent whine, such
loitering, shrugs of youth.

These Unaccountable Moods

Fitful wind harangues the hillside it loved once. Orchard bemoans its open-boughed ways, wants all its apples and best years back. Much on the mind in this squally twilight. My off-leash hound, because he can, chooses indolence, lags behind. Interstate unseen but lurking, a distant flute into the earth, immeasurably long. Trucks interminable out there. Haulage gravel. Destination some gray and brackish elsewhere that needs fill. I second-guess earlier moods, my trusted companion meanwhile gone cold equivocal beside me, though for reasons only a twitching snout can articulate. Windfall here anatomize in the sparrow-high cheatgrass, sweet-stink cloying as a carnival's sugar-dusted midway. I refuse my human urge to tally, to audit, or otherwise diminish every lungful of this late day redolence, this beautiful and troubled night, accountant of the wretched world between jobs that I am.

Trees Make You Think of Other Things

You never think of flowers
in relation to anything else, nor

even trees, though trees at least
seem to scaffold the sky at times,

(as if the particular vista you're
thinking of was a work in progress.)

And once, on a walk in the woods
with your father, you came upon

a rotted red oak—the old man's guess—
strewn over the two-track like a toppled

ghost. "Gypsy moths," he whispered,
fingering the gray bark with a reverence

the living world would never expect of him.
So: it seems that trees do make you

think of other things, and there are so
many of them—trees *and* other things—

that you begin to feel oppressed by
the incalculable intimations, the math

of associations, the cold roots, the leaves.

The Shadow Throwers

What rare perception do ants own
such that in their interminable marching
and conquering, the world is ever more
than its vast flora seas, its feasts
of dung beetles? The trails at my feet
are incalculable. Of those that lead
to temptation, a few are lined
with columbine and larkspur,
and lovely women wave from hilltops,
sporting daises in their hair. From
a distance, such paths lead to colonies
of light, particles and waves of bliss,
though closer up the shadow throwers—
absence, umbrage, heartbreak—say otherwise.

Provincial Cemetery with Figures

Light too earnest to bear when the clouds break.
Houses in the far hills suggestive of black

top-hats, formalizing the terrain's otherwise
sensible attire. At my feet these bronze

slabs, rows just symmetrical enough to prove
a human hand—plan instead of providence.

I remember I first came here out of loss;
as its lackey I return, again and again.

This aftermath seems all there ever was: swaths
of witchgrass and sage, the harried, elemental

silences of fields. And a two-track out of here
like penciled-in ruts in the landscape.

The few other visitors, figures strewn amongst
the dead, appear to have long ago plundered

futility's measly stores: laughter fidgets
about me now, barely noticed, like bashful

children. Nearer still, budding lilacs lick
the air with their jaunty, virginal tongues.

Stalled Trains at Paddock Street

Ore-humped hopper cars like serpents coiled and skulking whenever the Paddock Street gates stuck. Our sunup clothes ashy as ever and lunch pails metallic as tang the foundry cindered into local flavors. What waned and vanished we saw coming for miles. Where were the mothers we knew as ours? Absent, yet cinched to us like sallow cloth over naked tribal shame. Knuckles raw with wailing, your father ground stars. Mine whizzed through porch lattice into any rain. Their rightful places twigged by dim Paddock taverns. Hard rooms upstairs, some windows never painted shut. Those ledges the closest thing we had to birthright. Rain-mottled, pigeon-tarred, retched from morning, noon, and night.

The Cliff Divers of La Quebrada

Gnashed precipice,
and far below, the cove

of riotous sea into
which the young men

gaped (it seemed
lovingly) before

each immaculate
plunge. Afterwards,

dripping wet—out
of their depth—seven

clavadistas greeted us
with zip-lock tip bags

and the timorous grins
of the pitiable

as we made our way
back to the parking lot.

Looking Down on Tepoztlán

West of there a half dozen cumulus
huffed toward *la pirámide*

like brazen Mexican sons. Far
below, the valley town whose name

my *gabacho* mouth never learned to love,
seemed to have perfected the art

of inconsequence. It was market day
down there—fresh guava, lime, roses,

a thousand or so variations of chili
candies, silver keychains of sombreros

and soccer balls, wood carvings
and papier-mâché caricatures of old

Don Quixote and his pal Sancho, long
gone to seed in everlasting celebrity.

Two-Player Games

Night-fuddled, seeking asylum, now that God's teeth seem to grit each time he ponders you. Interstate in earshot of the old bank-barn, the pigswill, a few torpid swine sampling the late field-rot. You list, then right yourself like a fast-sobering drunk in the dank rain-fields. Already October under wing, south-wooed doves and red-winged blackbirds. Wood-smoke in the crags and clefts of hills out where the tar-shacked hermit lives. You hear him mornings on the slant road, wake to his gravelly slog. Once, you paid him to prune the wide-draped alder away from the house, to grease the whiny weather-cock. Later—a dream?—you invited him in, hauled out all your two-player games. Taught him what you could of Oklahoma gin, the vast intricacies of thumb warring, rock-paper-scissors, how to properly stalk a king.

After the Storm

These scoured rooms redolent
of mock lemon, dust chemically

unsettled in morning's water-
logged gleam, falling, rising,

maybe music if I could hear it,
like so many unheard things.

A plane in the sky overhead,
reverb of flight but also

of distances, goings-away.
Maybe you up there in coach

echoing the ardent thoughts
of your fellow travelers:

Can't get there soon enough.
Raincloud's view of the wide

world below, etched and grooved
and parceled out into wetted hues

according to plantings or wildness
or asphalt. Then a sharp wash

of light, unbroken heaps of cerulean
sky up ahead, all the old spats

and scraps cleansed away, our
life expunged as chemtrails.

Somewhere Between

Neighbor Bill's antibodies
mutinous, turncoat. The *C-word,*
say the two gray ladies

of the cul-de-sac. Helps explain
the visitors at all hours
coming and going, hushed

voices on the portico,
solicitudes wafting in the night air
thicker than moth traffic.

Six months left, sigh
the ladies, a year if they can
make his dying dawdle.

Brooding back to the house
I leave the ladies to esteem
pity's easy, suburban gait.

Home, my wife can't help
but agitate: *Don't those windbags
know that somebody's dying*

is none of their damned business?
I trace her shoulder
with a touch that has years

in it, that knows
there are worse things
than hedging bets.

A touch somewhere between
just let it go, and yes,
I know exactly what you mean.

No Rest for the Weary

Doomscrolling the night away
with a proper scowl and a lesser
regard for benign appraisal

than ruthless verdict, mystified
as usual by how everyone but me
has found a surefire way

to monetize their profligate
trash-talk, their raw coitus, making
mint out of the slip-shod, the nakedly

amateurish. Little by little my fears
and jealousies at this hour exceed
dignity's time-worn limits, outstrip

my once enviable knack for quashing
certain little sophistries of the heart—
and now daylight IRL clambering in:

nothing but decree, dawn's sundry,
onerous orders, most of which I will
refuse to unseal, let alone obey.

Testimony

Heavily the scarecrow leans
into the mazy maize sea, pockets

picked, zipper unzipped, button-
orbs unthreaded, drooping now

into endless cross-eyed gawking.
Yet nights like this of full-on moon

he can still make out the flight
of those hench-crows, those

dozen or so denials of light,
plumed buckshot splaying dread

and harm. Gang of thieves,
cawing toward dawn, black

as the robes of high tribunals
bored with the unanswerable.

Where It Hurts

Two floors above Mill Street rummies
thin pillows rarely oblige un-swilled heads.
You knew the policy going in. And late hour
pong of fried onions and soured breath.
The bright side you always used to see
no matter what catastrophe,
dimmed now, grimed over like the lone
painted-shut window. Flying dreams
all grounded: ceiling permanent zero.

And that woman loitering about? Heedless
(rumor has it) of unlovable men, or else
grown partial to rough-handed hankering.
What they say about her could fill
urinal walls, and somewhere does
if certain cratered men with venom
enough and a felt-tip pen told it false.

You've bought such exploits before,
knowing you could do worse—that vulgar
tune you trill. You're torn. Her scent sage
and sad, unfair to parade around in
if she's not looking for salve. You could
reach out and touch her where it hurts,
ask if she wants to come up. The barman,
neither Samaritan nor buttinsky but fair
tactician, mouths *Don't*. Pours.

The Fall

On some indeterminate edge
of Eden's shabby outskirts,
in an underlit diner

known for middling fare
and gravies that collude
with broken ceiling lights

to obscure the unsavory truth,
he picks a booth with a clear view
of the door, ready as any

sprinter out of the block
to make a run for it, which
is why he finds himself here

in the first place, having bolted
from every hissing hint
of desire he senses

slinking up on him—
or say the kind that comes
waltzing in just now

like a dive-prowling Eve
looking to lure her wary Adam
into taking that one big bite

he's been putting off
all night long, though in truth
his once boundless stamina

is waning fast, even as
nothing on the menu here
looks remotely edible,

and the gravies that help
everything go down easier
have all sold out.

Having Learned Nothing

Because in this dream
what is absent or mislaid
or stolen is unrevealed,
I suspect from the onset

that loss itself
is the crucial theme
on which I'm being tested.
Soon enough, strangers appear

en masse, delivered by
chartered bus to my door,
and like the often luckless
or seldom loved,

they arrive on scene
hackles up, ready-armed
with a keen sense
for the trouble at hand.

Before I can stop them
a prayer circle forms,
followed by the obligatory
hand-linked search through

a sodden, squally landscape,
twenty or thirty people
kitted-out improbably
in matching raincoats

and muck-boots, scouring
bramble and thicket,
not a voice raised above
a nervy whisper. Afterward,

the search party routed
by the dream's killjoy tenet
that any discovery must be
the dreamer's alone to make,

the busy-bodies start
to wander off in sulky pairs,
boarding the bus for the long
ride back to . . . where?

It's a question that gnaws,
even as I sense the liminal
geography, the not-quite-here-and-there
of it all, is beside the point,

little more than fungible sets
on the backlot of my subconscious,
where most of the odd characters
who come and go are day players

working for scale. Including, I
presume, the one who now sits in my
reading chair, made up to impersonate
my late father, his muddy boots

slung over the pouf ottoman
in a boorish pose so dead-on
Method I'm shocked when
he doesn't say, *Hey, numbnuts,*

get me a beer. Instead, he tells
me he's just grateful my dream
brought him here after hiding out
in the deep bramble for eons,

biding his time, watching, waiting
to be invited in and offered
a comfortable seat. He explains
that he once had a whole speech

memorized for this very scene,
but now the words won't come.
He wonders if I'd be so kind
as to feed him lines

from the aching soliloquy
I've often dreamt he would give.
Say, a few helpful hints at all
the bravura sorrys

I expected him to tender. Any
little bone I might throw his way
to help him faithfully deliver
each and every beautiful lie.

Doing Damage

Our long-cracked lives fused
again, we sampled this newfound
state called *not unhappiness,*
filling the house with the placid
sounds and manners of two
people paired off for the better,
now that what we'd learned to call
the worst was behind us. Many
nights, dodging the now censored
words, but still fumbling about
for the jargon in whose scrupulous
use we'd been so well edified,
we lounged in silence in our
deck chairs and watched the stars
up in the hills milling like shaft
miners at the drift. Other nights,
we listened hard while the anxious
mother next door called her two boys
inside, then heard their giggling
somewhere near, followed by their
hushed schemes to disobey.
Sometimes they laid low in our
pachysandra, or else ducked behind
the boxwood. A few times, playing
war with sticks—old enough to know
that doing damage was the point—
they even trampled our prized beds
of ornamental sage. We grumbled
but didn't really mind, intrigued by
the little footprints and broken flowers
morning would bring. Evidence
of trespass and fracture duly noted,
proof of the messy world still out there
beyond our walls, if not our ken.

Lucky Bastard

Admit to being only faintly rattled
by the world's nightlong terrors,
or at least not as much as decency's
shrill morning alarms would advise.

Concede, too, that you're never half
so haunted as the brigadier still grieving
yesterday's wanton, bloody battle
(even as he's plotting tomorrow's

righteous assault.) And though you
aren't above pretending otherwise,
fair to say your daily burdens hardly
compare to the those of the oncologist

who knows before the bloodwork is back
how God's fastidious handlers
sometimes keep our prayers from
ever reaching His weary ears.

Confess, finally, to the indefensible
transgression of always sailing
through, of never having any more
use for the soul's quotidian jitters

than for its infinite inane hopes, all
of which first require bearing the bruises
and cut-to-the-bone body blows only
the normal way of things can dish out.

So, please: give us hapless billions
out here—bogged down, fretful, waiting
for the other shoe to drop—a tiny peek
behind the curtain, a lesson in the art

of sleeping through every last, desperate
night, and maybe just one or two
of the cleverest tricks you know
to help us ply your insufferable trade.

Busted Compass

In a crowded room near midnight
surrounded by that over-served

and sanguine mob swearing like gurus
by their personal polestars and true norths,

and for whom apparently there exist
a million expedient reasons why

everything lovely or cruel happens to us,
you and I bumped into each other, not

(we could both agree) through fate's
ecstatic aims, but rather guided by

sheer indifference—the same old
busted compass we both swore by—

spinning us in blurred circles toward
that secret, beloved point on the map

otherwise known as neither-here-nor-there.
We hadn't talked or touched in years,

which might have explained why grazing
shoulders without warning left us dazed,

but also anxious to pretend we were
strangers enough by now not to relive

the ache of that time when touch
itself had become an accessory

after the fact to our chronic crimes
of the heart. We sat together then

on a worn-out sofa that ponged
like an eight-foot blunt, not *not* touching

while we waited for a few clumsy words
to muster themselves, those little

ill-trained platoons of language
that always mean well but never know

what to do when the shooting starts.
We distracted ourselves by watching

two people at the other end of the sofa
sucking on each other's faces so hard

we could feel all the air in the world
pouring past. That was us once, my smile

and nod tried to say, while your smirk
and shrug admitted you knew better than

to deny it. Then your biting (vintage) frown
warned me we shouldn't do this, it was

no use, just as your meager nudge
swore the time had come already for us

to go—as we always had, always
would—on our separate, fateless ways.

Shaping the Scene

Of late you can't help but notice
every mirror as you pass

getting harsher in their unbidden
reflections, so constant now

are their quick, implicit digs
squarely aimed at your buried id

though always feigned as misdirected
glare at your sneakers' scuffed

soles or threadbare laces, before
moving on to a few evident

if unfaced facts, such as your hands'
recent quivering or your brow's

years-long psychic rut. And it only
gets worse whenever you dare

linger, the looking-glass taking
its time sizing you up, only to dress

you down like every tormentor
who has ever enjoyed the meagerest

sway over you. Which reminds you
of an egotist friend who once claimed

mirrors only reflect back
the *strum und drang* you let them

and any harm done is wholly
reversable by looking away,

or better still by stepping off
to the side (which is merely stagecraft

and not, like shutting your eyes,
denial), allowing you to shape

the scene in a more favorable light.
Such as now, with its oblique portion

of your unmade bed, Rilke's *The Book
of Hours* tented on the nightstand,

each open and ready to slip back into
at any moment, and in the corner

the yellow moth orchid, a gift
you didn't ask for but now love

for the way it reminds you
there is at least one delicate thing

in the world that cannot thrive
without you. Yet the real star

of this *un*show is your own insistent
absence, the mirror's narrow aspect

a still life as if rendered by an artist
far more attentive to what is missing

and why. Say an artist literally after
your own heart, trying to reveal

by no small feat of blossoms
and the private inanimate

its frayed but ever beating contours,
to show how like the rest of you

it's not AWOL but near, buoyant
and maybe singing, just out of sight.

The Wars of Repetition

You're confused, she says.
But you're not, and you know
you're not. *You're* a thief,
you say, sure you gave her
a twenty and not a ten.
Her grin chides: *prove it.*
You turn to the woman behind
you in line, but those blue
bystander eyes shut you down.

Sometimes the shiftless world
and the straining soul converge,
and sometimes it happens
in a party store where you're
trying to buy a soda and an old-
school newspaper, the headlines
of which inform you that
three wars rage concurrently.
Get the manager, you say.

Reaching Shore

Some others standing
about like chessmen
in stalemate. Foothills
where all the campers'
litter flocks
become a high mantle
of gulls. Skies gray
scuttled battleship.
Wane of spindrift,
driftwood the busted
kneecaps of foul gods.
A bottle washed
ashore, the message
inside clear: *don't go,
wait right here.*

About the Author

Jon Ballard's poetry has appeared in *Cimarron Review, Flint Hills Review, Broadsided, DMQ Review, Valparaiso Poetry Review, San Pedro River Review, New Plains Review, Connecticut River Review, Midwest Review, Blue Earth Review,* and *The Great Lakes Review,* among many others. He is the author of five poetry chapbooks; a full-length poetry collection, *Possible Lives* (Kelsay Books, 2020); and a novel, *Year of the Poets* (Loose Leaves Publishing, 2014). He lives with his family in Michigan.

www.ingramcontent.com/pod-product-compliance
Lightning Source LLC
Chambersburg PA
CBHW030913170426
43193CB00009BA/827